GOING WOODARD

Communication. Connection. Change.

Carol Woodard

Copyright © 2020 Carol Woodard

All rights reserved

No part of this book may be reproduced, or stored in a retrieval system, or transmitted in any form or by any means, electronic, mechanical, photocopying, recording, or otherwise, without express written permission of the publisher.

ISBN-13: 9798551055297

There are people in life that become more than a mentor, more than a friend, they become your hero. I can never fully express the deep gratitude that I have for the man who blazed the trail of education and became the bright light on my journey, leading me down the path of my success. He told me the truth, told me to suck it up, and to move forward when obstacles blocked my path over the years. When I close my eyes, I can hear his Staten Island brogue telling me to stay focused, stay strong, and to never ever lower my standards. A man of great integrity and high education standards..... my hero, Michael Vanacore.

CONTENTS

Title Page
Copyright
Introduction
I Know But I Don't Know...   3
For the Love   6
Change- It's Not Nuts   8
Be-YOU-tiful   10
No Fear   13
Move Your Feet   15
Keep Jumping   17
Pick Your Pain   19
Destination: Amazing   23
Clear and Concise   25
Hearty   27
Attainable   29
Nourishing   31
Gaugeable   33
Exciting   35
See it to Achieve It   39
Believe It   41

Bank Experience	43
Brush off the Rust	45
Be a Good Follower	47
Putting it All Together	51
Bueller? Bueller? Bueller?	53
Programmed for Success	58
Don't Snap	60
Remember Ebbinghaus	62
Oh, Shift	64
Elevate to Motivate	66
Across Generations	70
The Baby Boomer	71
The Gen Xer	73
The Xennial	75
The Millennial	77
The Gen Zer	79
Afterword	83
Gratitude	85
Endnotes	87
Recommended Reading	89
About The Author	91

INTRODUCTION

Congratulations! You are well on your way towards something new! By simply purchasing and beginning to read this book, you have completed the first step towards change. You have shown that you have the desire, and you must have desire!

In my lectures, trainings and in this book, I use the term educator a lot. It won't take you long to realize that, to me, an educator is anyone who helps another human being to succeed. Within our schools, we have classroom educators, admissions educators, and financial aid educators. In life, we have individuals who educate others on which cable service is best for their needs, which foods are best for their health, which exercise programs are best to master, doctors who educate patients on how to regain their quality of life, and religious leaders who educate on salvation. We have mothers and fathers in our homes who educate their children on how to brush their teeth, drive a car, or how to score a date with their newest crush. To educate is to teach, and to teach is to educate.

My travels have taken me far and wide, to really big venues and to small private spaces, and the one thing I can tell you with 100% certainty is that it is not what you teach, but how you teach that creates desired results. When we connect with another human being, then and only then does the magic of communication come into existence. To learn to teach, we must first learn to communicate. If you are thinking, "yeah Woodard, this sounds great but what is THIS magic ingredient needed to create effective communication?", then let me tell you that it is as simple as making sure that you gain trust, that you really listen, and that everything you teach is to the maximum benefit of the other person.

Life is funny, people are funny, and communication is the one thing that heals wounds, strengthens relationships and advances careers. Explore your own hopes, dreams, and motivation before educating others. You don't need a degree or a doctorate, you just need grit, determination, and effective communication. No one listens to or trusts a hypocrite who talks the talk, but isn't willing to walk the walk. Change is hard, but staying in the same place and living with the knowledge that you could have had more if you'd only tried is far more difficult to swallow. You can wish in one hand and …well, you get the picture.

Enjoy the book! Oh, and don't forget to read it with a Texas accent!

GOING WOODARD

I KNOW BUT I DON'T KNOW...

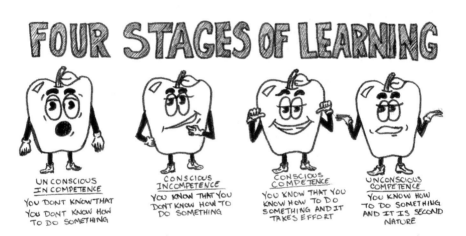

One of life's surprises for me was when I finally understood the madness of the four stages of learning. Funny how that goes, I had always known about it but like most things in life, it took a few trainings, book readings, and life experiences to REALLY fully get it. When my moment of understanding happened, I realized it was nothing more than a few simple concepts wrapped up in some really big words.

Stage One - Broken down, this does not mean that you can't do something because you are not smart. This just means that you can't do something because you did not know it was there to do. When you hear something for the first time and you get that rush of adrenaline and think, 'Really! How cool is that?! I can't wait to give it a try!'. How many times in life have you made the statement, "I would have taken care of that if I had known"?

Stage Two - My favorite. Now that you know about it, you realize that there is something you have not tried before. Challenge accepted! Let the learning begin! Now that you are aware, the responsibility shifts over to you to gain more knowledge. Knowledge brings learning and learning brings practice. Practice brings skill and skill opens opportunities!

Stage Three - Ahhhh, this is where you not only know the information exists, but you are also all over it! You know the information and have the skill to prove it. You're good and you know it. You are a pro!

Stage Four - This is mastery at the subconscious level. You know that you know the information, but you don't know why or how you know it. It might be something that you grew up doing, or shortcuts you have developed over the years with repetition. You are proficient in something, but seriously do not remember how you learned it. You are unaware of the how or when but have mastery of the doing. It comes to you naturally, like cooking or gardening. You really can't explain how to do it, you just do it.

Your audience will be in one of these four stages at any given time. Effective facilitators allow for natural transition among the phases as the information is received by the attendee. Whether it is in the classroom, boardroom, or the convention room, facilitators deliver information that hit different recipients at different levels - all at the same time. Being good at what you do means gaining knowledge you didn't already possess, applying the knowledge gained, and practicing the skills developed with an 'I can do' attitude. Great facilitators know it is up to them, as the facilitator, to impart the knowledge, wherever the learner happens to be on the scale.

As we continue to explore Going Woodard together, you will fall in one of the phases of learning yourself. Make notes on where you are and the opportunities to learn new skills that appear as you read. Get comfortable in your chair, buckle your seat belt, and get ready to read, learn and grow.

FOR THE LOVE

What comes to mind when you hear the phrase, "for love of the game"? If you're a boomer or gen xer, you might picture a hunky #14 on the pitcher's mound. Others might think of late evenings watching game tapes or early morning workouts or Friday nights under the lights. Personally, I can't help but think of my now grown daughters who played tennis competitively throughout high school and college. They played after school, on weekends, and whenever they could in between. We hauled them and all of their stuff all over the state to compete in tournaments, even during the summertime, neither of them ever seemed to want to take a break. Both dreamed of going to college on full scholarships, becoming world ranked players, and competing at Wimbledon. As soon as my youngest completed her collegiate career, however, she put down her racquet and never picked it up again. She hasn't stepped on a court in nearly 20 years, doesn't know who's ranked first in the world, and has no idea who won Wimbledon last year. Why?

When she first began to play, she'd practice day and night. Not because she had to or needed to, but because she wanted to. She'd choose to spend her weekends and summers on the court because she enjoyed it more than going to the mall or seeing a movie or going to the community pool. We wore the suspension out on our family vehicle hauling her from one tournament to another, weekend after weekend, all over the state of Texas. The dynamic changed for her though when she went to college on a full athletic scholarship. Suddenly she wasn't just playing for fun, she was playing for tuition money, meals, and the ability to attend an expensive, out of state university. She was no longer playing for "love of the game", and the thrill of the game was no longer her prime motivation. In order to pay for her books, she had to pass a physical. To have enough money for tuition, she had to maintain a winning record on the court. The game wasn't so much fun anymore as it was her job. She no longer spent her weekends on the court- when she came home, her racquets stayed at school. When tennis was in off-season, so was she. Her passion for the game fizzled and the fun fizzled out with it.

Why do you get up early every morning and work late every evening doing what you do? Is it so you can pay your rent or is it because you have a burning desire to succeed? Do you still find fulfillment in your work as you did when you first began, beyond just staying out of the red each month? Is there joy in what you do or are you just doing enough to get by? Are you working your profession or is your profession working you? If the fun has fizzled for you, it has also fizzled for those who look up to you. It is time to reevaluate your game plan.

A phrase many of my past and present students like to use in reference to my class is, "it's time to Go Woodard". We are passionate about keeping learning fun in my classes, not only for our students, but also for ourselves and we like to keep things exciting! So, join us as we bring back the love, and make learning fun again.

CHANGE- IT'S NOT NUTS

The world dynamic is constantly changing, and if we are to be successful entrepreneurs who love what we do, we must continuously change alongside it. Be weary of change that looks too good to be true though. If you are looking to take the easy way out, it might just cost you!

We could all learn a lesson from the quick and agile monkeys that lived in the jungles of Africa. Hunters tried and repeatedly failed for years to catch them because the monkeys were just too quick and agile to pin down. Then they discovered a fatal weakness- the monkeys really, really (really) liked nuts. The hunters began stuffing nuts down into narrow-necked soda bottles which they then chained to trees. The monkeys would wait for the hunters to leave, and then slide their open hands into the bottle thinking they'd hit the nut jackpot, only to discover that they were unable to remove their hands once fisted around the nuts. Quick and agile, but also horribly stubborn, the monkeys would refuse to let go of their prize. They would then be easily captured when the hunters returned and found them still attached to the bottle chained to the tree. I know what you are thinking- these monkeys sound nuts!! All they had to do to be free was to let go! But the uncomfortable truth is that these animals were actually highly intelligent beings. Part of the reason that they were so difficult to capture using conventional hunting methods was because of how easily they could outrun and outwit their captors! But why scavenge for food when they have delicious nuts just sitting right there? Isn't it better (read: more comfortable) to work with what you already have as opposed to risk exploring other options, even if it isn't currently working out well? Do you ever think, "if I just sit here long enough, this problem/issue will resolve itself with time?". And what if there aren't other nuts out there? There were guaranteed nuts right where they were. Truth is, even if the hunters hadn't returned, the monkeys would have still been chained to a tree, captured by their own fear and lack of ambition.

Are you learning to adapt to the ever-changing landscape of life or are you stuck in a rut, watching as the energy and excitement fades away? Do you have heart and the desire for better things, but are afraid to let go of what you already have? Don't be a stubborn primate. Open your hands, let go of your preconceived ideas (but keep hold of this book!) and embrace change. Don't remain chained to your previous methods, hoping things will improve on their own. Let go, open your eyes to, and have faith in the possibilities that surround you.

BE-YOU-TIFUL

A little note on change, before we really get going. There is a fine line that can often blur when we begin to change our methods that can lead to an identity crisis at our core. We see a successful person with a job we want or the life we think we want, and we try to copy them in our own thoughts and behavior. While we are all the same in that we have the same basic anatomy needed for survival- ideally, my heart pumps the same as yours, my stomach churns like yours, my nerves fire like yours, and so on- we are strikingly different at our core. How many times have you tried to be the crazy extrovert to get someone's attention when you're really the "my cat is my best friend" introvert or vice versa? How did that work out for you? Even identical twins who share the same basic DNA have differences at a genetic level. When it comes right down to it, no two people are completely alike. It makes sense then that there would be differences in how we process and apply information, and that those differences are why we fall flat on our faces when we try to be people we're not. Therefore, the foundation for our success must be based on the truth of who we are, not a pretend version of ourselves.

My older sister and I are only a few years apart in age. We went to the same school, shared the same group of friends, liked the same boys, wore the same clothes... you get it. Being older gave my sister an advantage, however. She wore makeup first, dated first, and learned how to make her hair stand up higher than the topping on mom's famous mile high meringue pie first. I hated it when she started going out with friends after school and I had to stay home by myself with my unmade face and flat hair! For a time, it appeared that she had everything I wanted but as we grew up, I realized that I wasn't much like my big sister at all. Turned out, I didn't really want to go out late with my friends, I wanted to spend my time at baseball games with my boyfriend, Mark (Lord help my sweet father), and I wasn't nearly as fond of hairspray either. We were both married as adults, had kids, grandkids, and rocked our own separate lives with our own families, doing our own thing but while still being close to one another. She would go on to have a successful career early on in her children's lives while also fighting for better treatments for her son with spina bifida, while I chose to remain home with my girls and help provide care during the day for my special needs nephew. Then I would return to the workforce later in life, as she retired to help care for our aging parents and her grandchildren. We both contributed to the world in ways that neither of us could have done had we not been ourselves and had I insisted on having everything she had and doing everything just as she had done it.

Who do you look up to and want to be? A sibling, parent, pastor, friend, or celebrity? I have bad news for you, and it's the only time I'll ever say this, but you can't do it. You can't be that person because you are you. And guess what? The world needs that little bit of you that only you can do. Improve your relational skills and self-talk, take better care of yourself- yes. Don't be afraid to make positive changes, but be true to who you are at your core. Strive to become the best you because you are amazing and only you can be you and do what you are meant to do. YOU are worth the work.

We've all heard of a certain bell tower in Pisa, Italy. The Leaning Tower of Pisa, or simply The Tower of Pisa, was built over a span of nearly 200 years. It's a hugely famous tourist destination, but not for the reasons the original architect had intended. It boasts seven floors and seven bells and a beautiful circular shape that was uncommon to buildings during that time, but that's not why people flock to see it. When the tower was first being built, the soil was weak and unstable and as the second story was added, one side of the tower began to sink. So, instead of simply being a magnificently beautiful circular tower, it is a magnificently beautiful ciruclar tower that leans at such an angle it looks as if it could topple over at any moment. People don't flock to hear it's seven bells, they come for the selfie. If you try to build on an unstable foundation, you too will begin to sink and your growth will be stunted. As you flip through these pages, be sure you are building your success on a foundation firm in truth and are remaining true to you.

NO FEAR

You've got a firm foundation and the will, so what's holding you back? We often think of fear as the ultimate dream crusher, the stubborn bouncer standing between us and our destiny. But what if I told you that fear doesn't have to be your enemy? Take for instance this story of two farmers discussing their upcoming crop that's been passed down through our family. We liked to tell this story to our daughters when they were facing a big tournament and were afraid of failure, and they still use it today to encourage their children with school. The story starts out with a farmer, who is sitting on his porch when another farmer comes to visit. The first farmer asks the second farmer how his corn is, and he answers that he didn't plant any this season because he was concerned about the crows ruining it. The first farmer then asks about second farmer's wheat, and he receives a similar response- the second farmer said he didn't plant any because he was too worried about weevils. So, next he asks about his potatoes, to which he receives another similar answer- he didn't plant any of those either because he was afraid of bugs. After a bit more questioning, the first farmer began to realize that the second farmer hasn't planted any crops and would have no harvest at all! The first farmer scratches his head and admits that he, too, was afraid that bugs and crows would ruin his crop, but that he had put up a scarecrow to scare them away, and he had found a safe insecticide to protect his potatoes and wheat. He had made adjustments because he was afraid, and guess what-- his crop was thriving!

Can you imagine how the second farmer must have felt at that moment? He thought he had sat out the game with fear by choosing not to play by not planting a crop that year, but really fear had taken him for all he was worth. He had absolutely no crop and no profit. Fear had blinded him.

Have you ever allowed fear to sweep an opportunity out from under your feet? Have you ever been so afraid of failure that you decided not to even try? Perhaps you didn't apply for a promotion you were qualified for because you thought someone else had a better chance of getting it or you've never learned to network at company get togethers because you are shy and afraid of putting yourself out there. Then 2020 arrived, and you really weren't sure if you'd ever get back out there ever again? We've all been there. You are not alone, but if you are sitting around, waiting on a better set of circumstances, you are wasting valuable harvest time! The problem isn't a bug riddled field! The problem is an inability to manage fear, and the solution is within reach!

Where would we be as a civilization if we allowed fear to steal our opportunities to learn and advance? Would we have ever steamed across the Atlantic, or even have thought we would someday be capable of putting over 44,000 passenger planes in the air daily, jetting passengers all over the world to accomplish various tasks? Can you imagine how frightening the idea of flying 40,000 feet above the earth in a steel shell would have been to someone living in the nineteenth century, before the Wright brothers took flight? But the Wright brothers didn't let fear ground them, instead they made elaborate plans for planes that could stay upright in the air in light of the risk presented. They proceeded with caution. With great success comes risk and with risk comes fear. Inevitably, you will experience it at some point in your career. Choose to use fear to your advantage by learning to appropriately determine and prepare for risk or allow fear to empty your field. If you do not manage fear appropriately, it will manage you!

MOVE YOUR FEET

"But, Mrs. Woodard. You don't understand. I'm not afraid, I just can't physically can't do it!". I've heard this more times than I can possibly count. As much as it sounds like an excuse (in all fairness, it often is), sometimes there is merit to this argument. Sometimes, we (or our students!) actually believe we cannot do things because of how we've been taught or what we've been told by a well meaning educator or mentor in the past. But oftentimes this is simply a teacher or employer's own insecurities, unknowingly or not, projected onto their students or employees. It reminds me of a story Joel Osteen of Lakewood Church in Houston, Texas tells about a German Shepherd who was hit by a car while pregnant. The German Shepherd was able to drag herself from the roadway after being hit and survived, but her hind legs were mangled and badly injured. For whatever reason, her legs were never set properly and when she had her pups, the owner noticed that they couldn't use their hind legs. They would drag their legs behind them when they walked, just like their mother. The owner took the pups to the vet to see if there was anything that could be done to help them walk properly and was surprised when the vet told him that there was nothing to be done. That he couldn't help at all. The reason? There was nothing physically wrong with the pups' legs!

Did you grow up believing that you are broken? Unfixable? Mangled and unable to reach your full potential? Perhaps it was something someone you trusted said that made you question your ability or something they did. Maybe it's simply something you think you see in others that you don't see when you look in the mirror. Something you think they were born with, something you simply do not have and cannot learn. We have a tendency to believe what we repeatedly tell ourselves!

What do you model to your students? Are you dragging your feet and do they drag their feet in response? Ouch. That's a gut check, right?

The good news though is that, unlike the momma dog, our legs aren't actually broken. Tired, maybe. Discouraged, possibly. But not broken. Maybe your last mentor was a real downer or you've been in quarantine so long without any motivation that you have grown used to sitting still. Maybe you haven't been the most energetic mentor to your students or employees. But guess what? You don't have to continue to sit on your butt! Your career can still be fun, energetic, and productive. You can still right the ship and make a difference! Once we realize where we are dragging our feet, we can choose to pick them up, walk in confidence, and model that behavior for our students! Be creative! Have fun with it. Use those legs your mama gave you!

KEEP JUMPING

Unfortunately, while we can strive to maintain an internal positive attitude, we cannot control how others respond to our successes externally. There will always be some negativity within our environment that is beyond our control. There will always be someone or something somewhere that will make us feel like dragging our feet. We can, however, control how we choose to talk to ourselves! We've often set the tone for our day before we've even had our first cup of coffee, long before our co-workers, peers, children, or students can influence it. When you find yourself stuck in a pit, who will be the first (and possibly the only) person to lend you a hand? (Hint- it's you!!)

How are you supposed to be your biggest cheerleader, even when you aren't feeling it? How quickly do you give up when faced with a seemingly insurmountable challenge? Imagine this- there are a group of frogs hopping through a forest and two fall into a pit. The other frogs gather around, see how deep the pit is, and determine there is no hope of rescue. They yell down to their friends that it is pointless to even try jumping out of the pit, and that they should accept that death was imminent. The two frogs have nothing to lose by trying, however, so they start to jump as hard and high as they can. Their friends yell from the top of the pit, pleading with them to let go and to accept their fate. The first frog makes one final jump and gives up, falls deep into the pit and dies. The second frog, however, continues to jump and jump, in spite of his friends' pleads and cries. Finally, he jumps just high enough to grab ahold of the ledge and pulls himself out of the pit! His friends are thrilled but also a little dumbfounded and ask, "couldn't you hear us? Why didn't you give up?!!". The frog answers, "I can't hear you! I am deaf!".

Have you ever woken on a Monday just not feeling it? Walked into the classroom or an interview on a big day with fear and trepidation instead of hopeful anticipation of how you will perform? Do you put a smile on your face, give yourself a quick kick in the rear, and refuse to quit jumping? Or do you sit down and give up? How do you motivate your students when you aren't sure you fully believe in their abilities to succeed?

The deaf frog kept jumping because he BELIEVED his friends were enthusiastically encouraging him by their frantic actions. He made it out of that hole because he was inspired and motivated by his friends' belief in him. It didn't really matter what words were being spoken, but how they were delivered. Truth is, we can be our own best ally in encouragement even when we feel more like the enemy by choosing positivity over negativity. Positive self talk isn't just about words. It's an energy, a feeling that you allow to bubble up from within- even when you don't feel like it! We can extend that to our students as well by remembering not to give empty encouragement. When you support your students, make sure there is energy behind it!

PICK YOUR PAIN

My youngest daughter is a bit of an introvert. Her first response to the frog story was that she'd prefer someone toss some food and water down into the pit over her having to jump out of it. She's fairly certain she could live there happily if she didn't have to make small talk with anyone and Starbucks would still deliver her coffee fraps. After COVID-19 forced a nationwide shutdown in the spring of 2020, and she was basically able to put this ideal into practice though, she realized it wasn't that great after all. Although she didn't want to hang out with everyone all the time everyday, she still needed in-person interaction with humans who were not related to her, (particularly ones she did not birth). Virtual meetings in her pajama pants were great until Spring Break ended and virtual public schooling began, and it was nice not being expected to be at awkward extended family fuctions, but she missed seeing her immediate family, too. As it turns out, she likely would not have enjoyed being in that hole longer than a day or two! So, whether she gave up or tried to jump out of the hole, she would have experienced pain. The same is true for you. You must pick your pain, whether you try or not.

My husband and I live right on the outskirts of Dallas-Fort Worth. We face two major decisions every day- which route we should take to work and which route we should take home. DFW is often ranked as one of the top cities with the most congested traffic in Texas, and is reguraly in the top ten in the United States, and top

30 worldwide. Each route has its pros and cons- some are frustratingly slow yet simple enough to require very little brain power, while others are faster yet more complex and require more careful navigation. It's a pain either way we go, we just have to decide if we're willing to risk the complex yet shorter route or if we would rather inch our way forward absentmindedly with the rest of the crowd.

We make a similar choice as educators and entrepreneurs. Are you hesitant to allow technology in your classroom for fear that you will get lost or have you ever decided against using a new business strategy because you're simply too mentally exhausted to implement it? You are not alone. It has been estimated that over 40% of first time teachers will leave the profession in five years' time due to teacher burnout, and only 15% of employees feel engaged at work worldwide. There are various reasons for this, most of which you probably have all experienced at one time or another- low pay, long hours, high stress, poor student behavior, lack of support, interpersonal conflict.... the list goes on, and these numbers are likely change for the worse with the unique challenges the COVID-19 pandemic has brought into the classroom. But there is one simple reason that seems to receive very little attention that might actually surprise you. It's boredom! Yes, you can be swimming in a sea of tasks and paperwork yet still be bored by a lack of creativity.

As a successful entrepreneur, you must pick your pain. You can choose to take the easy route and experience the eventual pain of burn-out, or you can choose the more complex route and experience the pain that comes with change and growth. You can face the heartache of coming to hate what you do, or you can roll up your sleeves, wipe your brow, and grow to love it. Which do you choose?

Yap About It
Thoughts and Takeaways

1. Ouch! Something that hit a little too close to home:
___
___
___

2. Woah! Something new I learned:
___
___
___

3. Yay! Something I can change today:
___
___
___

4. ADDITIONAL NOTES:
___
___
___

CAROL WOODARD

DESTINATION: AMAZING

Congratulations on making it this far. I'm so excited that you have decided to pick your pain and commit to change. There will never be a better time than right now! You have the will, the desire, the strength, and are ready to bring about positive changes in your life. That's amazing! Now we just need to decide on one minor, tinsy tiny detail- where do you want to go?!

Would you get on an airplane with no flight plan or onto a cruise ship with no set course? Of course not. Not only would deciding on a destination en route create confusion and division among the passengers, it would also waste two very valuable resources- money and time. Of course, having a predetermined destination doesn't mean that you can't change course mid trip due to unforeseen complications or changed circumstances, but you need to know the direction you are going and what you want to achieve if you expect to arrive there in a reasonable amount of time.

We've all heard of the five year plan. It's even possible that you've dated someone with a five year plan and really want to punch me in the throat right about now. That's okay because I'm not suggesting you develop such a plan. Exactly. What I am suggesting however is that you dig in deep and search your soul for what it is that you really want out of your career, and start thinking about what you are willing to give up to get there.

To arrive at an amazing destination, you must put in an amazing amount of work. Have no doubt, there will be sacrifices, let downs, and bad days. But if you are willing to do what it takes, there will also be victory.

So, what are you waiting for?! Let's get started. Are you ready for CHANGE?

CLEAR AND CONCISE

First things first, your goals must be clear and concise. You need to know exactly what you want and when! The more general your goals are, the harder they are to measure and to achieve.

I have five grandchildren. My youngest three, all boys, live three hundred miles from me. Every summer, they each get to come for a week-long visit by themselves, without their brothers or parents. They get to choose what we do and what we eat and where we go. When my ten year old grandson visited last summer, he said he wanted to make a cake from scratch while he was here for his summer birthday. He had never made one before and thought it would be a fun activity to do together. The only problem was that his Mop hadn't made a cake in about 20 years or so and really had no idea what she was doing, but he's cute, so we did it anyway. When he got into town, we went to the store to gather supplies. Once we were on the baking aisle, we realized just how far in over our heads we were. Did you know there are different types of flour? Self rising, not self rising, bleached, non-bleached, bread, cake, almond, coconut... it was enough to make our heads slightly spin. Once we decided on a bleached white flour, we moved on to the fats section and realized we didn't know if we needed oil, shortening, butter, or some combination of all three. And sugar- was it granulated or powdered, and white or brown? Did we need baking powder or baking soda? Iodized salt, sea salt, or kosher? We hadn't even made three quarters of the way down the aisle before he decided that he had changed his mind and wanted a bakery made cake after all. He gave up on his goal before he'd even cracked his first egg. Where did we go wrong?

Clearly, our plan needed a plan. We had the vision and timeline, but lacked direction. Saying that we were going to bake a cake and planning to do so by going to the store for supplies, then going home and baking it wasn't sufficient. Our plan needed more meat. My grandson's homemade cake was doomed from the moment we stepped into the store without a list.

Does your plan have a plan? Have you done your research, and do you know what you need to get to where you want to go? Don't venture out unprepared. Be clear in what you want and as concise as possible in how you will achieve it.

HEARTY

What comes to mind when you hear the word hearty? Personally, I think of really good stew. Yum. But did you know that hearty can also be used to mean a vigorously cheerful person? Like, "Jon gave a hearty smile to his teacher, Bob (thumbs up for Jon!)". Here I mean it in a combined sort of way- your goal should be hearty and full in that it should be concise and meaningfull, and you shouldn't short change your ability, but also hearty in that it should be something that you are vigorously cheerful about.

John Scolinos was a 78 year old retired Cal Poly Pomona baseball coach when he gave his well-known speech, "17 inches", in 1996. He delivered the first several minutes of the speech with a home plate hanging from his neck, not mentioning anything about it until about 25 minutes in, when he asked the audience if they knew how many inches a standard home plate measured in little league. Someone answered that it was 17 inches, and so he moved on and asked if anyone knew what the standard was for high school baseball? Turned out it was 17 inches, too, and so he continued to ask, making the rest of his way through college, minors and majors. They all gave the same answer- the standard sized home plate measures 17 inches in every league, no matter the age or skill range. That is the accepted size and the range that every single pitcher has to throw over. If a pitcher is unable to throw within that range, a lot of different things might happen- the player might switch positions, or be put off the team- but the one thing that won't happen? The plate won't get any wider.

My girls were young when Nolan Ryan threw his 5,000th strike out but they both still remember watching it on TV at their grandparent's house. No one there could possibly forget the energy and excitement of that moment (some of you Millennials and Gen Zers are just going to have to take my word on this one). But I can only imagine how different things had been if it had been decided ahead of time that Ryan would receive an extra inch or two on to his strike zone. It definitely would have taken some of the anticipation out of the moment for the fans, and I can imagine, for Nolan as well. And while throwing 15,000 strikes across a 18 inch range isn't exactly a small feat in and of itself, it wouldn't have been nearly as exciting.

Don't sell yourself short by widening the plate, even marginally. Be clear about what you want, and go for it wholeheartedly.

ATTAINABLE

While you shouldn't sell yourself short, your goals should also be attainable. Now, am I doing an about-face and telling you that you can't do something? NO. But if your goal is to become President of the United States and your only experience in politics is that you ran for class president when you were eight, then we've probably still got some work to do on setting smaller, more attainable goals.

Did you know that Oprah started out in local radio or that Ralph Lauren started out in the fashion industry as a clerk who sold ties for men? Both are now hugely successful, but neither became an icon in the entertainment or fashion industry overnight. Lasting success takes dedication, hard work, sacrifice, and time. Keep this in mind when you are setting your goals.

We are cat people. When my girls were growing up, we'd have anywhere from two to four to five cats lounging on the back of our sofa at any given time. Rufus, Wolfer, Willie, Butthead… just to name a few, we had quite a tribe! The girls loved playing with the cats but learned early on that in order to keep the cats' attention, whatever toy they were playing with had to be held within the cat's grasp initially. For instance, if they were playing with the cat's fishing pole, they had to hold the plush fish close to the cat's face and allow it to swat it a few times before lifting it above the cat's head. Otherwise, the cat would look at the swinging fish high above its head, cut its losses and simply move on to chasing after easier things, like the cat who lived in our full length hallway mirror.

We, ladies and gentlemen, are like cats. We don't like working for things that are far beyond our reach. If the reward is great enough, we might try for a little bit, but we will all eventually either get bored or fed up with the disappointment and give up. Like the cat, we need a reminder every once in a while of how being victorious feels. As you are making your goals, be sure you are giving yourself that opportunity by making smaller, stepping stone type goals designed to get you to where you ultimately want to go. To be successful, we must feel successful.

NOURISHING

"Do what makes you happy."

It's on bumper stickers and Tshirts and those cute little wooden block signs people put on their countertops and desks. At face value, it seems like a fairly fool-proof agenda to live by. Who doesn't want to be happy?

At the time this book was being written, COVID-19 hit our community hard, and we were put on lockdown. My husband works in the medical field and so he continued to work full time throughout the quarantine and I was home alone. Typically, I am out of town more often than I am at home and am not used to spending my days inside my house by myself. Sitting on my butt in my living room binge watching every show my daughters recommended and sweeping the house repeatedly did not make me very happy. What made me happy was going on my one essential grocery shopping trip per week. What would have made me really happy though would have been to jump into my Mop mobile and go spend a week or two with my grandchildren. If I were living by the above agenda, I wouldn't have even bothered to ask for permission. I would've just shown up with my bags packed and a week's worth of candy for each kid!

There is a difference between doing what makes you happy though and doing what keeps you well nourished. Going out of town to stay with my daughters and grandchildren during a nationwide stay at home order wouldn't have been good for my health, no matter how happy it made me. So, when I say that your goals need to be nourishing, I do not mean that they simply need to make you feel good. I mean that they need to be good for you. Feelings are fleeting, but the after effects of true nourishment are not.

Your goals need to inspire growth and strength. They need to draw out the good parts of your character and propel you forward. If you hate small talk, a lucrative yet commissions based sales position might not be the best fit for you. If you hate animals, maybe don't plan on becoming a vet or opening your own dog walking business. But, on that same note, just because you enjoy small talk doesn't mean you'd like selling life insurance, and just because you have fourteen cats (and counting!) doesn't mean you'd enjoy a career as Dr. Doolittle either. You have to find something that makes you feel energized beyond your surface. Your goals shouldn't just hold the promise of making you momentarily happy, they should be life-giving.

GAUGEABLE

Back in the 80's and 90's, traveling was quite a bit different than it is now. When we took our young girls on a road trip to the coast or up north, we'd have to buy a map and draw out our route ahead of time. GPS was not around to tell us when we had missed our turn or how many miles we had left or when our estimated time of arrival was. If we made a wrong turn or missed our exit and couldn't quite figure out where we were on the map, we were at the mercy of an attendant or cashier at the gas station where we'd ultimately stop to ask for directions (after making sure we were actually for sure, 100% lost). The kids would occasionally ask if we were there yet. Then came the internet and step by step directions that you could print and take with you. These cut down on ,but did not eliminate, the stops to ask for directions, and our teen girls asked a bit more frequently when on earth we would flippin' get there. Now when we travel, we have smartphones and GPS and turn by turn directions in real time with a constantly updated estimated time of arrival based on our current speed. We ask Alexa or Siri for directions and the grandkids ask EVERY OTHER MINUTE what our newly estimated ETA is, even when we aren't traveling far enough to use navigation and have no idea other than, "a few minutes". I'll admit that it annoys me but I can also understand why they continue to ask because I find that I am always checking myself when I am a passenger. Knowing where we are and how much further we have to go is comforting to me, and I also find that I am less frustrated on longer drives. Back in 1990, our girls would ask the same question but with less frequency because they knew the information wasn't available. Our grandchildren, however, know we have that information right at our fingertips. While I didn't worry about it with my own children, when I take my grandchildren on long car trips, I ensure they can see the GPS screen so we can all have a peaceful trip. They are much calmer when they can gauge where they currently are, where they are headed, and when they expect to arrive there. Also, knowing when we've hit important points along the way, such as halfway or a certain landmark, gives us something to celebrate along the way!

When I know exactly where I am going and how much farther I have to go until I arrive there, I feel much more in control of my situation. If I need to stop to take a breather, I can feel confident in doing so and in being able to recalculate my ETA. If I'm not making good time, I can adjust my speed, and if I begin to divert from my path, I can quickly get myself back on track. The same is true for our goals. If we are keeping track of our progress, we can recognize and celebrate whenever we make gains and also be aware when we are falling off course. If you haven't already done so, write out a copy of your goal and put it up somewhere you can see it as a reminder of where you are going and where you currently are on your path.

EXCITING

You've searched your heart, discovered your desire, and have set a goal. Are you excited? You absolutely should be. If not, you might need to go back through the previous sections and reexamine how nourishing and hearty your goal is. Because it's time to use that excited energy to move forward!!

If you haven't already, write down your goal by hand. This is very important. Typing it out will not give you the same type of experience, and you will miss out on the increased neural activity to the brain that writing by hand produces. So, no shortcuts here and no tablets, laptops, or phones. I'm talking a sheet of paper and a pen, y'all. Archaic, I know.

Now, write down what it is that you want, when you want it by, and how you intend to get it. For example, if I were wanting to

Hang this paper up somewhere where you will see it everyday. This might be on the inside of your medicine cabinet, on your bathroom mirror, maybe even on the inside of your car visor. It doesn't really matter where, as long as it's somewhere you will see it regularly so that you can read it aloud to yourself as a reminder of what you want to help keep yourself on track.

After you've done these things, it's time to share your goal(s) with others. Accountability can be key in keeping course. Tell a loved one or close friend or mentor what is up and what you are doing. Be sure to choose someone you can trust to be supportive and honest regarding your plans. Be clear in what you expect from yourself and how they can help you stay focused and on course.

Yap About It
Thoughts and Takeaways

1. Ouch! Something that hit a little too close to home:
___
___
___

2. Woah! Something new I learned:
___
___
___

3. Yay! Something I can change today:
___
___
___

4. ADDITIONAL NOTES:
___
___
___

CAROL WOODARD

SEE IT TO ACHIEVE IT

We've got the desire, the will, and a destination in mind but how do we get there? What if our personal circumstances are less than desirable for professional growth?

Have you ever found yourself facing a situation that seemed impossible to escape from unscathed? Like life had you by the thumbs, and you were completely powerless? My grandson, who we nicknamed PH, has had brain surgery. Twice. I have never felt so powerless as I did on the days of his surgeries as the mother to my daughter. All of the usual uplifting pleasantries were out the window. There were no bright sides or silver linings, and no one wanted to be thankful that it wasn't any worse because, to be frank, no one wanted to think about such things on that particular day. When people ask her how she was able to wait through her son's brain surgeries, her answer is always two-fold. One, what else was she going to do? Two, she put in her ear buds and imagined she was anywhere but in a hospital waiting room waiting on a surgeon to finish operating on her son's brain.

My daughter didn't know it at the time, but she was tapping into a method used by Viktor Frankl, a Holocaust survivor and neurologist, during his imprisonment in Nazi concentration camps. I came across his story while reading Stephen R. Covey's "The 7 Habits of Highly Effective People", and it mesmerized me. Mr. Frankl suffered unimaginable loss during this time, losing his wife, mother, father, and brothers. He himself did not know from day to day when, or if, it would be his turn to die. His body was completely and utterly broken from beatings, starvation, dehydration, and abuse. He and his fellow prisoners were treated with extreme disdain and neglect. One day he found himself naked and alone in a cell, and realized that every last thing had been stripped of him except one thing. The Nazis could take his freedom, his family, his clothes, his livelihood, potentially even the air from his lungs... but they could not take his basic identity. Being a self-aware being, he could use his imagination to transport himself from the concentration camp to a future lecture hall full of students where he wasn't a starving prisoner but a healthy, well fed professor. He also learned how to use this self-awareness to choose how the torment of the camp would affect him emotionally. These were things in which the guards had absolutely no control. He realized that even in the midst of such deplorable conditions, he still had the freedom to choose how it would affect him mentally and emotionally. He inspired other prisoners within the camp to utilize their own self-awareness, continued his career as a successful neurologist and psychiatrist, and also became an author after his release.

You cannot choose what life will throw your way and you cannot control how the world will treat you, but you can control how you respond and whether you will use the energy tossed your way negatively or positively. When the world says to give up, push back. When the world says, there is no bright side here and nothing to look forward to, pop in your ear buds and refuse to believe it. It's your choice.

BELIEVE IT

There is a folklore legend that has been making the rounds since the mid 1900s about a Vietnam POW who sat in his cell every day and played golf mentally for several years. The details vary in each re-telling, but the outcome is the same- he found after release that his golf game had improved a great deal and credited the time spent playing imaginary rounds of golf in his head for his improved stroke.

The POW isn't alone in his success. Comedian Jim Carrey spent hours in his car parked on Mulholland Drive in Hollywood visualizing his success for years before his acting career took off, the Seattle Seahawks used visualization to prepare for Super Bowl XLVIII, and Arnold Schwarzenegger has reportedly used the power of visualization in his bodybuilding career, acting career, and as a politician.

How does this relate to you? You don't have to be in prison or in the Super Bowl to use the power of visualization. This tool is free and available to every sound and open mind, no matter your position or walk in life! It can be used in a variety of circumstances, from every day matters to major, life altering scenarios. How and when you use it is completely up to you. Every sound mind has the tools they need to achieve their dreams!

Tips:
    1. Find a quiet, private place where no one will bother

you.
2. Sit and close your eyes.
3. Create a detailed image in your mind of the environment in which you will be competing or presenting. Pay attention to detail. The more senses you engage, the better.
4. Imagine the event starting, progressing, and then what it will feel like when you are victorious. See, smell, feel, and taste the victory.
5. Practice, practice, practice. The more often you use visualization, the better it will work. Don't wait until the day of a big presentation, game, or interview to begin. It is most effective when used weeks or even months in advance.

As with most things in life, the power of visualization becomes more evident the more we use it. If you don't feel particularly moved after the first few times of trying it, don't give up. It takes time and practice to learn to clear your mind and really focus on what you want, and this will take a bit of troubleshooting and trial and error. You might find you are more successful in a certain room or chair, or perhaps during a certain time of the day. Just keep trying until you find your sweet spot!

Learn to change the photo reel in your mind from your failures to your future successes. If you can SEE it, you can BE it.

BANK EXPERIENCE

What if I told you that in addition to using powerful visualization methods, there is another technique that you can use right now to help propel you towards your goals and prepare you for success-- and that you already have this tool at your disposal right now? That there is absolutely nothing you need to change to use it, other than to recognize its existence?

"We have a problem". This is not a phrase most business leaders or educators want to hear but one we will all undoubtedly hear it at one time or another. These problems can be serious enough to prompt group brainstorming sessions, late night phone calls, and long meetings, but they are rarely emergencies. Our solutions are usually well thought out and deliberate. How you respond to less emergent problems as a leader, however, impacts how you will respond in an emergency when you must make a sudden decision on behalf of both your business and clients/employees/students.

When a flock of geese flew into the engines of US Airways Flight 1549, Captain Chesley "Sully" Sullenberger III didn't have time to consult the Airbus operator's manual or to seek the recommendation of the National Transportation Safety Board . He had to decide right then, at that very moment, whether to attempt a five minute trip back to New York City's LaGuardia Airport or to make an immediate, rough landing on the Hudson River. His passengers didn't have time for critical thinking and brainstorming, he had to make a sudden decision. In an interview with Katie

Couric following the accident, he said, "One way of looking at this might be that, for 42 years, I've been making small, regular deposits in this bank of experience: education and training. And on January 15 the balance was sufficient so that I could make a very large withdrawal"[1]. Are you banking experience by learning from your mistakes or are you avoiding conflict? Can you be trusted to make a sound decision when you don't have time for deep thinking? Would your employees/clients/students agree?

Don't dismiss everyday problems as unimportant nuances. Embrace conflict for the learning opportunity it is, so that when an emergency strikes, you are ready. Don't dwell on the negative, embrace the positive. You will make mistakes but you also will learn from them. Recognize conflict as an important part of your own education and training, and use it as a tool to help you reach your goals.

BRUSH OFF THE RUST

 Believe in yourself. Set attainable goals. Bank Experience. All of these things are important, but we are still missing a fairly big piece of the Going Woodard game plan. If you are truly going to see change and measurable progress in your career, continued education is a must.

Russell Herman certainly had the will for change. Herman lived in Southern Illinois and became well known publicly following his death in 1994 at the age of 67. He was featured in numerous news articles, including one written by Wes Smith in the Chicago Tribune entitled, "Will Power". Herman had a will, you see, that left a hugely generous amount of money to several places in need- over six trillion dollars in total to the state of Illinois, the United States Forest Service, and the US government to help pay off the national debt, among other places. He would have forever been remembered as a man that provided a great financial service to his city and country had it not been for one minor detail- when he died, he only had one asset, a 1983 Oldsmobile.

The face value of Herman's proposal looked great. I can't imagine that the national forest service would have said no if approached with such a proposition! What about the promises that you have made to yourself in your life? Your dreams, your goals, your aspirations? Those promises look great at face value, right? But what happens when things don't go as planned or when you face tough challenges? Do you have a garage full of newly learned, innovative tools or outdated, worthless strategies? Do you have the tools needed to fight back when life throws a wrench in your plans or do you just have a rusty old car that no one drives anymore? If your garage is full of outdated trash, it does no one any good.

Herman certainly had the willpower, and arguably, the heart to bring about change. What he did not have, however, were the necessary tools to put such change into action. Having good intentions is not enough, we must continually strive to better ourselves and keep our tools up-to-date. Otherwise, all we have is a lot of good ideas and a rusty old mess. We are never so wise and so good in our field that we cannot learn something from someone else. There is always, ALWAYS something left to learn and somewhere left to grow!

BE A GOOD FOLLOWER

If your plans involve moving into a leadership or management position, this is especially important. To be a good leader, it is essential that you first learn to be a good follower. Helping your audience learn to be good followers will also help them become more accomplished leaders in time.

No one thinks to themselves in kindergarten, "someday, I want to be an entry level employee!" or "I want other people to tell me what to do, and I want my livelihood to depend on it!". Right? We all want to be leaders, but rarely do people start out at the top, and there is good reason. Many attributes shared by successful leaders are learned as followers. Here are three things you learn as a follower that help you become a more successful future leader:

You learn to pick your battles. Is what you are hearing meaningless chatter that can safely go in one ear and out the other or is it something that can potentially sabotage the team? Should you attempt to de-escalate the situation, escalate it by taking it to a supervisor, or try to halt the rumor mill by ignoring it? As a leader, you will hear it from all directions. Your inbox is always open, and messages are constantly flowing in, whether they are direct messages, snide remarks, gossip, even negative looks and vibes . You must learn to filter out the trash so you can focus on the problems with potentially real consequences for your team and or product, and not waste any of your or your team's time and energy on trivial things that will eventually self resolve anyway.

You learn how to read people. Introverts. Extroverts. Millennials. Gen Xers. We are fond of labels, aren't we? These labels can certainly be helpful but knowing how to read people individually is still an absolute must. People cannot be broadly placed into categories. There is not a one fit all. You'll likely offend the Baby Boomer on your team if you assume they can't use social media or hurt the introvert's feelings if you ignore them because you assume they don't want to make small talk. Learning how to read people quickly and efficiently is an incredibly useful tool as a leader and being part of a diverse work environment is great practice!

You learn to think for yourself. A good leader delegates out pieces of the puzzle or problem to followers to individually work on, and then helps arrange the solution. As a follower, you must think critically on your part and as a leader, you will use those skills to help decide who to delegate which task and how to bring it all together. Critical thinking is, well, critical. You must first learn to think for yourself before you can think critically on behalf of a group.

Whether you are working your first entry level job with dreams of becoming CEO, or are the CEO, these traits are important for your success. Learn to successfully follow and boost your leadership potential!

Yap About It

Thoughts and Takeaways

1. Ouch! Something that hit a little too close to home:
___
___
___

2. Woah! Something new I learned:
___
___
___

3. Yay! Something I can change today:
___
___
___

4. ADDITIONAL NOTES:
___
___
___

CAROL WOODARD

PUTTING IT ALL TOGETHER

Do you remember how you felt the first time you fell in love? Do you remember how the first few days/weeks/months felt versus the last few? When something is new, it is exciting and fresh and we don't mind if we spend all our time doing one thing only because we love it and it's exhilarating and we don't want to do anything ever again! Then the newness wears off, the momentum shifts, and it isn't as fun. Then it shifts some more, and it can become no fun at all. We have to work to keep the momentum flowing in our relationships.

The same can be said for our professional endeavors. What seemed to be an exciting career in sales can turn to long, boring days at a call center, a class might be exciting on day one, only to sour by the second week.

I give a talk to educators on how to keep the spirit alive in the classroom called, "Bueller, Bueller, Bueller". Sometimes we need to spice up our self talk and expand our experiences to keep ourselves motivated, and sometimes we need to initiate change and spice up our teaching to keep our audience engaged. As we become more excited and more focused and more inspired to reach for our goals, we can funnel that excitment through to our audience and/or students! If you are a Gen Zer or younger and have no idea who this Bueller guy is, do not stress. Continue to read on, and I promise it'll come into focus.

BUELLER? BUELLER? BUELLER?

Most of us are familiar with the scene from Ferris Bueller's Day Off, where the teacher is trying to get the attention of high school student, Ferris, in a comically even and monotone voice. Perhaps we've never been quite as tedious or dull, but we've all been the teacher trying to reach the student who would rather be anywhere else but in our classroom. We've stood at the front of the room, book in hand, attempting to relay important information to help the student do well in a field that they have personally chosen to enter, information that they have likely gone into significant debt to receive, only to be met with blank stares, hair twirling, and empty seats. We have the information they need to succeed, and yet they seem uninterested. Why?

Imagine you have been listening to the same person speak for over an hour. It is so quiet that you, and everyone else in the room, can hear your growling stomach. You want to pay attention but you can't help counting the tics of the clock and wondering how much longer until lunch (dinner, break...). You're hungry and you've lost all feeling from the waist down from sitting in the same position in the same plastic chair for what seems like forever. You have felt your phone buzz two or three times and you're wondering if everything is okay out there, but you aren't brave enough to quickly sneak a peek. Because you've been sitting so still, you have also seemed to stop producing body heat. So now you are freezing, hungry, worried, and you can no longer feel your legs, toes, or the tip of your nose. You could make a trip to the restroom to attempt to regain feeling in your limbs, but that would mean using your one socially acceptable bathroom break. What if you have a legitimate need for the restroom later? People begin to think weird things if you excuse yourself more than once in one sitting. Too risky. You stay in your seat but you're long past benefiting and learning from whatever you are trying to listen to.

There are lecture halls spread across every college campus in America. Students sign up out of obligation and for the credits, but no one actually wants to take a class that meets in one. The larger the room and the more seats it has, the less enticing it seems to become. It's no wonder though, whether it's a rebuking type (uh oh, someone's in tr-uh-bull) or simply informative, no one wants to be on the receiving end of a lecture. It doesn't matter how interesting the subject matter is or how important it is to our education and/or livelihood, we're going to have a hard time sitting still, listening, and not thinking of the other one hundred thousand million things we think we need to get done that day. We are accumulating unread texts and emails, some of us really important people might even have missed phone calls. Is it rude to stand up and stretch? What if I just take a quick look at this email to make sure it isn't an emergency? Was that thunder or the a/c? What are we talking about again?

Change is hard. By nature, we are creatures of habit. We like our routines and life is easier when things stay the same. The problem though is that we can miss out on chances to make life better by resisting change. Most of us have heard the Jon Bon Jovi song, "The More Things Change" and are familiar with the idea it proposes, "the more things change, the more they stay the same". In some aspects, this is absolutely true. You should not, however, use it as an excuse not to change! Think of it as improvement instead. You aren't changing the material you are teaching, you are simply improving its delivery and absorption. For instance, if I order something from an online retailer and I don't have a membership, it's going to take up to 4-5 business days to arrive. If I have a membership, I might get it for free in two days. The retailer didn't change the product I'm receiving but instead improved it's delivery while increasing the chances that I'll remember, and seek to repeat, the experience.

So, what other forms of teaching are there aside from lecturing? You can role play. Use simulations. Utilize anything that engages the student directly with the information you are presenting. Skip the whiteboard and use a visually appealing Powerpoint presentation instead filled with photos and videos in place of long, boring paragraphs or textbook quotes. Encourage group discussion and do class projects. When you don't allow or encourage your students to participate, you are sending the message that they are not valued in your classroom. In addition to including them in classroom discussion, give your students small jobs and let them help you run the classroom. When students feel valued and needed, they will feel as if your class is theirs, too. Maintaining passing class test scores, keeping an acceptable attendance record, and starting on time will become a shared responsibility, instead of yours alone. Develop a class motto or a mission statement. Encourage collaboration among your students. Let them work in groups. Once they have ownership of and feel pride in the classroom, you won't need to teach them to be a responsible student. It will come naturally.

On that note, let's talk about technology. Most of us aren't as comfortable with technology as our students and most of us feel like we still have a lot to learn. So, if the teacher is uncomfortable using something, does that mean it shouldn't be used in the classroom, no matter how valuable of a tool it is? In this case, the answer is definitely no. Most students can type faster than they can write, so allow laptops or tablets for note-taking. I know you're thinking they'll just end up online, but the benefits outweigh having to set and occasionally walk the room to enforce those boundaries. Don't be afraid of the smartphone, utilize it! It's okay to learn from your students. Ask if there are any apps relating to the material or education in general that they are using that might be beneficial to share with the class. If there is something you want to incorporate but you can't quite figure it out, ask! Don't hesitate to use your students' experience with technology to the benefit of you and your class. Let them teach you and they'll not only be engaged, but they'll feel valued, too.

Change has a habit of bringing chaos wherever it goes. So, let's talk a little about personal grounding. I don't mean preventing shocks from static electricity or finding your place in the universe, I mean staying grounded or anchored as the leader in your classroom. When I suggest that you share ownership with your students, I do not mean that you should give them control of the class. Those are two separate entities. The person who controls the class does the delegating. They give out tasks and share insight with their students, but they also oversee the run of the class as a whole. Do not lose sight of that vision. If your students value your relationship enough to trust you with their life secrets, that's fine, but do not unload all of yours, whether at school or not. Share with them classroom responsibility, sure, but do not burden them with your personal life drama. They do not need to know the details of your date last night and that you swiped right when you really should've swiped left, that your aunt's second cousin has cancer, or that your cat died when you were eleven and left you with an emotional void but that you find the strength to move on by the joy you feel in teaching their class. Encourage them, yes. Drown them with details from your personal life, no. You also should not be spending much (if any) time outside of class socializing with students. Don't go to the bar after school or to the party on Saturday night. Say this with me, "I do not need a relationship with my students outside of the classroom to make them feel valued inside the classroom".

Socrates said, "the secret of change is to focus all your energy not on fighting the old, but on building the new". Let go of tedious lectures and embrace group learning. Don't be afraid of technology or of learning from your students. Classes should be fun, animated, and full of student participation. Delegate responsibilities and let your students share ownership of the classroom, but maintain creative control and stay personally grounded. No matter where you are in your curriculum, it is never too late to change. Starting today, you can make the rest of your class the best of your class. Don't just lecture. Engage!

PROGRAMMED FOR SUCCESS

The human brain is often compared to a computer. The nerves act as communication pathways and synapses as circuits. We all have the same basic hardware- two hemispheres, four lobes, cerebellum, brainstem, white and gray matter. Yet what works for one student won't work for another. Some learn best with visual input, others need auditory input. Some learn better in groups, others do better with a textbook. Our heads are filled with the same structures and gray matter, so what gives? Like a computer, we might have the same structures on the inside, but we are all programmed with different software.

No two students or audience members will have the exact same processing system. Even siblings brought up in the same home, who went to the same school, and had the same parents are equipped with their own unique software. Maybe one was better at sports and grew up hearing "you are so good at {softball, baseball, football, etc}" but was never told how much potential they had off of the field, too. Maybe a teacher once told them they weren't smart or a coach told them they were too slow. For better or for worse, we have a tendency to internalize whatever input we receive from authority and adjust our behavior (output) to match what we believe is expected from us. A student who thinks they know everything might actually not think they know anything at all and the participant who acts too cool to participate might actually be afraid to speak up. The good news though is that, unlike a computer, we don't have to respond the way we've been programmed to. We can write our own software and choose to delete the things that keep us from reaching our potential.

My grandson was delayed developmentally. His teachers voiced concerns about a lack of social skills early on. He spent a good chunk of his elementary education hiding underneath his desk. He made great grades and read at a seventh grade level by grade 3, but wasn't expected to participate or add much to the classroom discussion because of his past social behavior. That changed when he started fourth grade and his teacher told him that she didn't care what his previous teachers said, she saw his potential and believed that he would make friends and do well in her class. It took him a few weeks to come out of his shell, but he eventually stopped hiding underneath his desk and even joined an after-school club. He didn't know that he was capable of making and keeping friends because no one had ever expected him to be able to. His fourth grade teacher changed that by giving him the confidence to hit delete. She changed his "I can't" into an "I can".

Encourage your students and particpants by pointing out their potential, not harping on past failures or potential limitations. Don't just tell them to reach for the sky. Believe that they will do it, and they'll believe it, too.

DON'T SNAP

My oldest grandson took a year off from cross country to be in the school band. He was visiting our house at the end of the school year and said, "Mop, I don't think I can go back to running. Every time I run more than a few steps, I think I'm going to die!". I feel his pain. Do you?

I'm not talking about running specifically, although it is possible that I would actually fall over and die if I ran for any amount of time whatsoever. I'm talking about endurance in the classroom or workplace. The stamina needed to make it through an entire year of repeated questions, assignments to be graded, paperwork to be completed, emails to be answered, lesson plans to be written, a seemingly never ending cycle of getting up early and staying up late with swollen feet and an aching back... well, you get it. Work is hard, which is why caring for our personal health is a vital part of our continued success and absolutely necessary if we are to be able to continue to persevere in our classrooms.

Have you ever stretched a brand new rubber band beyond its capacity and had it break on you? It hurts! Rubber bands start out stiff and inflexible- they need to be worked in a little before you can really stretch them. If you ask too much too soon from a rubber band, it will come back to bite you, quite literally. The same can be said for our flexibility in handling everyday stress. My grandson will return to cross country this coming fall, but only after he stretches back out a bit. He's going to have to start running laps this summer until he can build back up his endurance and ability to run longer distances. Otherwise, he could snap and injure himself and not be able to run at all. And if I ever decide to take up running, you can be assured that I won't be starting out with a marathon!

How do you unwind and stay flexible? Whether you use something as formal as progressive muscle relaxation or as simple as listening to upbeat music, be sure you are being intentional in your self care and setting manageable, stepping stone goals. It is important to both your success and overall health, and it is also important to your students' or audience's success. Your students look to you to help them gauge how the mood will be for the day. If you come into the room flustered and moody, they will feel flustered and moody. If you don't feel like working, they won't feel like working. If you come in energized and ready to take on whatever punches the day throws at you however, they will be more likely to be willing to jump in the rink alongside you. If your students are inflexible and unmoving, evaluate your own flexibility and self care regimen.

REMEMBER EBBINGHAUS

If you have ever attended a training of mine, then you know I am an "education hog". I love to take online courses in hopes of finding a new golden nugget of information to share. I have taken courses, however, sometimes even for months, and walked away with little or even nothing to share. Late one night, after a long day and with a very tired mind, I was finishing up a module on a course that I felt was going to be yet another one of those, 'nice to know but not anything groundbreaking' adventures when BAM, information was presented about the Ebbinghous scale. My blood started to pump and my mind started to race as I soon realized that I had found my golden nugget.

The more I read, the more I wanted to vocalize my thoughts, "Yes! That's it!". My life as a teacher was unfolding in front of me and my biggest dilemma was being explained to me via a computer screen during an online course by an instructor that I had never even heard of before!

One of our biggest challenges when delivering information, whether in a classroom or an auditorium filled with entrepreneurs, is how to ensure our audience is receiving the information that we are presenting with staying power. How do we help them with recall? Why do they pretend they are hearing things for the first time when we have delivered the information on multiple occasions? Helloooooo, Ebbinghaus!

Hermann Ebbinghaus was one of the first to make a connection between learning and retention. He put the puzzle pieces together. Looking at the Ebbinghaus remembering curve was like a light bulb moment for me. When delivering information, the key to remembering is repetition, something I had known all along. Yet, it took the work of a hundred year old gentleman wearing a monocle to open my eyes to the power of it. What the Ebbinghaus scale tells us is that the follow up is equal to or more important than the initial delivery. It is like potty training a toddler. You tell them, show them, and remind them; not once but every chance you get until they have accomplished the feat on the subconscious level. Check out the scale and tell me that it is not amazing!

Ebbinghaus Forgetting Curve

* Day One — 100% information recall
* 24 hours — 20 -30% information lost
* 48 hours — 60% information lost
* 1 week — 70% information lost
* 1 month — 80% information lost

Taking a weekend workshop is great. Reading this book- AMAZING. But you need to do more than just listen or read the information once. The same with your students, the information must be re-represented for maximum learnability. Otherwise, by the end of month one, up to 80% of the information you have worked so hard to teach and/or learn will have been lost. Thanks to this handy scale, we now know that follow up is key.

Hermann, where have you been my whole life?!?

OH, SHIFT

"It's not what we say but how we say it". This is something that we have all heard before. We hear it and move on down the communication highway without really thinking about what it means. Have you ever made a statement and then had it come crashing back down on you, like a ton of bricks? If you are a teacher or facilitator, have you ever had someone complain that you are rude or uncaring and yet, you honestly can't figure out what it was you said to cause such a reaction in them?

Tone, pitch, and body language speak louder than our words ever will. I remember a time when my mentor, Shelton Ogle, told me that the students could hear me roll my eyes all the way from across the building. I thought, "What? Me, Carol Woodard, an eye roller?! Surely he is mistaken!". But then I started feeling self conscious and decided to ask my family and trusted friends if Shelton's assessment was in fact correct. The results were unanimous and not exactly in my eyeballs' favor, which I knew meant that I either had to change my "eye language" or get creative with some stylish sunglasses for indoor wear. Darn it!

Being made aware of this made me work at stopping a negative behavior that I didn't even know I had. How you think determines your actions, and awareness is the first step to bringing about change. I had to become aware that the thoughts behind my eye rolling episodes were speaking louder than my words. I began to take note of what my mind would say as different individuals would talk to me, and I found that my thoughts ranged from, "Geez Louise, I don't have time to listen to you!", to, "OMG-really!?!", to, "I was always told that there are no stupid questions in the classroom but WOW!". Yikes, no wonder my eyes were betraying me. This began my NLP journey.

If you have ever been in a live training session with me you know that I am a NLP or Neuro-Linguistic Programming nut. My family will tell you that I don't just do things, I DO THINGS. "All the way or not at all" seems to be my motto. Determined, I did not take one course on NLP, I took two. I did not do the forty hours of clinical work, I did eighty. I dove headfirst into the sea of body language and learned that our thoughts control our bodies, literally. If I had a bad day and felt picked on or felt loved, happy or sad, it all happened because of my thoughts.

When we stand in front of a classroom, a group of classmates at a high school reunion, members of the church, or on stage, what we think rules our outcome. I challenge everyone reading this book to get the guts to ask yourself the question, "what is it that I think about?". Realizing that you can change your life by changing your thoughts is one of the most liberating experiences of my life. I took the challenge and created a shift in my thinking. How about you? Are you ready to shift your thinking and your life?

ELEVATE TO MOTIVATE

"Mrs. Woodard... but, I'm so tired. My cat has a cold and my grandma broke her foot and my pet lizard lost its tail and then my phone died so I *barely even made it here*. I just can't *life* today!"

After 20 plus years in education, I really have heard it all. I'm often asked, "How do you motivate difficult students to work?!". Here are a few tips I have used throughout the years!

Don't use fear to motivate. Fear is a great motivator, only it's not. It is true that it gets the adrenaline flowing, our bodies decide whether to fight or flight, and most students will choose to stay in a class they are already invested in financially... but it can also cause psychological paralysis and it can prevent your students from completing their best work. And in the long run, power gained through fear does not last. If you want your students' lasting respect, it's best that they respect you as a leader because they respect your choices as an educator, not because they fear you.

Know your students. Set an example for your visual learners. You can tell a visual learner all day long how to do something, put it on an audio loop even, but they are not going to get it until you find a way to make it visual for them. Do it too overtly, they'll feel patronized, and your introverts will recede back into their shells. But offer a subtle example meant for everyone and they'll take notice without offense.

Help your students set goals, and celebrate their achievements. Set a class goal for study hours, or an upcoming test or quiz. Plan a small reward for when they meet their goal, let them know that you believe in them and expect that they will achieve their goal. Don't make them afraid of letting you down, but instead build up their confidence that they WILL succeed.

Encourage! Give your students a pat on the back (proverbially, if needed!) and tell your struggling students that they are capable of turning it around. A struggling student can ask for encouragement in the most annoying of ways. The class clown might just be really goofy, or they might really need some help but be afraid to ask for it! The student who won't make eye contact with you might be legitimately bored by the class material, but also might just feel ignorant for not getting it. Ask if you can help or encourage them to seek help elsewhere, but let them know that you see them and it is important to you that they succeed in your classroom.

Lastly, if you are struggling with teaching, it's time to set some goals for yourself. Be your own class example. Turn it around, celebrate, and give your students the desire and confidence to do the same.

Yap About It

Thoughts and Takeaways

1. Ouch! Something that hit a little too close to home:
___

2. Woah! Something new I learned:
___

3. Yay! Something I can change today:
___

4. ADDITIONAL NOTES:
___

ACROSS GENERATIONS

From the high school graduate to the empty nester, our classrooms and audiences represent a wide range of generations. There are the Baby Boomers, who grew up watching I Love Lucy on a single family TV; Generation Xers, who grew up begging for their own landline; Millennials, who lived for calling their friends for free after 8; and Generation Zers, who basically came out of the womb posting selfies. To reach such a diverse group, we need to learn about their generational experiences and differences so that we might bridge the divide and develop a plan that works for all of generations, but first we must have a basic understanding of their similarities and differences.

THE BABY BOOMER

History
Boomers are a product of the post WWII birthing boom. The Andy Griffith Show and Gilligan's Island were favorite television programs, and popular movies included Little Women and Westside Story. They lived through the era of the Civil Rights Movement, the assassination of John F. Kennedy, the Beatles, and the rise and fall of Elvis Presley. They were born during the time of Woodstock and the Sexual Revolution- the normalization of birth control, the increased acceptance of couples living together before marriage, and the challenge of traditional sexual behavior. It was also a time of political unrest with the emergence of the second phase of the Cold War and US involvement in the war in Vietnam. Famous Boomers include Tom Cruise, Elton John, and Oprah.

Characteristics
Boomers earned every honor they received growing up and they have an incredible work ethic as a result. They are strong team players but prefer to communicate person-to-person (a Boomer might be willing to talk for hours on the phone, but they aren't likely to remember the class-wide text you sent last week). You will find that family frequently comes first with a Boomer- they often have a different perspective on family, one that isn't always neccesarily better, but is definitely different than that of younger generations. Also, when they commit to something, they do so

completely.

In the Classroom
Let me tell you something- we have really put our Boomers to the test this year! 2020 has not been an easy year for the technically challenged. Yet, I fully expect to see them adapt and thrive, just as they did when we first brought in laptops and mobile phones into the classroom. You can engage your Boomers through icebreakers and open discussion, but they tend to speak in facts rather than from emotion. They can also seem all-knowing, but sometimes claim to know how to do something without actually being able to do it, so allowing extra practice time can be helpful. Boomers thrive on personal interaction but will not always respond well to feedback. Don't be intimidated if your authority is brought into question. Instead, assign them a special task to help them feel valued.

THE GEN XER

History

Generation X is often referred to as the "lost generation", between the well-known Boomers and Millennials. Born between 1981-2000, they grew up listening to Nirvana, Smashing Pumpkins, and REM. With mothers returning to the workforce, children from this era are known as "latch key kids"- they walked themselves to and from school or the bus stop with a house key around their neck and they were trusted to do their after school chores and/or homework before their parents arrived home from work. Most Gen Xers were in their 20s before owning a "car phone" (picture a clunky- yet foldable!- cordless phone with an extendable antenna) and in their 30's by the time the smartphone became popular. They are the most educated generation with a significant percentage having gone to college. They watched Melrose Place, Friends, and can do the Fresh Prince's Carlton like it's nobody's business. They saw the Challenger space shuttle explode on live television, lived through the Watergate scandal, and cried with the Boomers when John Lennon was assassinated. Famous Gen Xers include Will Smith, Leonardo Dicaprio, and Lance Armstrong.

Characteristics
As a result of their childhood freedom, Gen Xers are self reliant and might not have great interpersonal skills. They can be inpatient and cynical. They are highly adaptable though and informal in nature. They are more technologically capable than Boom-

ers, but might not be as proficient as younger generations. For this reason, they are often apprehensive about Millennials entering the workforce and fear they will be replaced or rendered useless.

In the Classroom
Gen Xers are skeptics in general, so be prepared for lots of questions- they will often want to understand the relevance of an assignment before completing it. Get their attention by using pop culture examples and visual appeal. Allow them to work in small groups but firmly stick to deadlines (a Gen Xer will not appreciate a last minute extension when they've already worked to make the original due date). Gen Xers respond well to continual feedback, so offer comments and constructive criticism often. You will find your Gen Xers adapt more easily to a virtual classroom than your Boomers, but might need additional help with newer applications and are less likely to be as comfortable with the newer social media platforms as younger generations.

THE XENNIAL

My youngest daughter was born in the early 80's, but she refuses to be grouped in with Millennials. In her defense, she did learn to type on a typewriter as opposed to a PC and didn't own her first laptop until college. She can use a library card catalogue, knows the difference between the white and yellow pages, and writes in cursive. She wouldn't know which way to swipe if her life depended on it, but she's also too young to be a Gen Xer. So, where does she fit? The answer comes in the form of a newly formed micro-generation called the Xennial generation.

History
Xennials were born between 1977-83 and fit snugly between Gen Xers and Millennials. Like Gen Xers, Xennials grew up in a non-digital world. They didn't text their friends, they called from a landline, and they weren't constantly being photographed or videoed by a parent with a smartphone. However, most middle class families had a family PC with a dial up modem by the time Xennials were in their mid-teens. So, while they might have had a digital-free childhood, they were introduced to technology early enough that they are able to navigate it like they grew up with it. Most Xennials will still prefer a text to a phone call or an email to a face-to-face meeting, but they also recognize the benefits to meeting in person (but only occasionally).

Characteristics
Xennials are cautiously optimistic. They are old enough to viv-

idly remember the events of 9/11, but are too young to remember the aftermath of the Cold War. They know all of the words to Ice, Ice Baby but also love them some Bruno Mars. Like a Gen Xer, they believe success is best earned through dedication and hard work, but they aren't against cutting corners and becoming an overnight success either. Unlike a Gen Xer, a Xennial does not worry about losing their job to a more qualified Millennial, but they also don't expect to become CEO within the first year (or maybe even ever and they are ok with that). If the Gen Xer is a cynical realist and the Millennial is an expectant optimist, then the Xennial is a realistic, ever so slightly cynical optimist.

In the Classroom
An Xennial brings the best of both the Gen X and Millennial worlds into the classroom, but they can also be difficult to motivate. Financial security is important to them, but not to the same degree as a Gen Xer. An Xennial wants to do what they love, but they also want to be paid well for it. They aren't likely to be willing to give up their happiness for more money or vice versa. Xennials did not grow up receiving participation trophies, but they do value achievement awards. Expect your Xennials to respond well to personalized recognition and to strive to be the best whenever a prize or award is on the table. An Xennial might not strive to change the world, but they will work really, really hard for a Target gift card.

Expect your Xennials to have fewer questions than your Boomers and Gen Xers if the need arises to switch to a virtual platform, but don't expect them to be as proficient as your Millenials and Gen Zers. However, since many Xennials were exposed to a digital world from as early as the later part of their teen years or even earlier, they should be quick to adapt. Encourage your Xennials to be their personal best and watch them bloom!

THE MILLENNIAL

History
Millennials were born between 1981-2000. They were the first generation to fully appreciate reality TV such as Jersey Shore, COPS, and Survivor. They jammed to pre-2007 Brittney and had pin-ups of Justin Timberlake taped to their walls long before he became a Man of the Woods. They went in droves to see Titanic, the Hunger Games, and Twilight (Team Edward for the win). They watched news broadcasts with their parents on the Oklahoma Federal Building bombing, Princess Diana's death, OJ Simpson's murder trial, and the Rodney King riots. They are old enough to remember where they were when the Twin Towers fell on 9/11 and were likely still attending public schools when the massacre happened at Columbine High School. Most had a cell phone as a teenager and upgraded to a smartphone in their 20's. Famous Millennials include Mark Zuckerberg, Taylor Swift, and Justin Bieber.

Characteristics
Having grown up with Google and a personal computer at home, Millennials are experts on technology. They are goal and achievement oriented, learn well from failure, and love to collaborate with others. They'd rather be broke and love what they do than become rich doing something they don't enjoy. A Millennial wants to make a difference.

In the Classroom
Millennials have a shorter attention span than their Boomer/

Gen X classmates but are very good at multitasking. They learn quickly and can swiftly move from topic to topic. Show videos and include viral news to get their attention, and use group activities and open discussion to keep their attention. Avoid anxiety and conflict by allowing the Millennial's constant companion, the smartphone, in the classroom (with restrictions as needed). Keep their attention in the virtual classroom by incorporating the use of smart phone apps in your cirriculum. Have them make and share videos or slideshows. Get creative!

THE GEN ZER

History

Generation Zers are children of Gen Xers and grandchildren of Baby Boomers. Born in 2001 or later, September 11th is something they learned about in history class at school. They've seen their fair share of violence and social unrest, however, being exposed from an early age to social media and online news. A large percentage grew up with either a smartphone or tablet always in hand, whether it belonged to them, an older sibling, or a parent. They've never had to navigate the dewey decimal system at a public library, use a payphone, or check messages on an answering machine. *69 means nothing to them (stop giggling, Gen Xers) as they've always had caller ID. They don't see technology as technology, it's just a way of life that they are well accustomed to.

Characteristics

While a Millennial regularly manages up to 3 screens, a Gen Zer can manage up to five simultaneously (TV, laptop, desktop, tablet, iPod/iPhone). They are used to having information thrown at them all at once from different sources and they are very good at managing it all. Managing a vitrual classroom enviroment would be no trouble at all for a Gen Zer. They are internet savvy, social media experts, and hyper-aware. Gen Zers are also very entrepreneurial. It's been estimated that approximately 76% of current high school students wish they could turn their hobbies into a job and 72% want to start their own business.

In the Classroom
Time for a single question pop quiz. Are you ready?!

1. How long is the attention span of a Gen Zer?
A) 30 seconds
B) 2 minutes
C) 8 seconds
D) What was the question again?

The correct answer is C (unless you are a Gen Zer, then the answer is a most definite D). Keep their attention by incorporating the use of tablets and smartphones in class. Focus on helping them turn their hobby into a career. Do charitable activities. Remember, a Gen Zer doesn't just want to make a living, they want to make an impact on the world. They don't just represent the future- they are changing it!

Yap About It
Thoughts and Takeaways

1. Ouch! Something that hit a little too close to home:
___
___
___

2. Woah! Something new I learned:
___
___
___

3. Yay! Something I can change today:
___
___
___

4. ADDITIONAL NOTES:
___
___
___

AFTERWORD

I truly believe that we all have within us the power to help others change their lives and the course of their family histories when we teach. A pinch of this and a little pinch of that, mixed with your gift of teaching is what makes the world of education spin. When one person grows, the whole world grows. Simple…right? Not so much. All things worth having come with a price. You will be tested as those who came before you were tested and those before them. I want to leave you with the words of Viktor Frankl, "When the test of life comes…success or failure is determined by how we respond". My hope for everyone who is willing is that you find your niche, that place of true peace.

Never underestimate the power of an educator!

~Carol

GRATITUDE

We all have moments of gratitude in our lives. I am grateful for my gift of teaching and for those I get the honor of educating. I hope you found the golden nugget you were looking for when purchasing this book. I enjoyed writing it, and hope you laugh as I did at re-telling many of the stories. I do need to thank my "fab five", who have supplied me with such wonderful material. Addie, Annie, Michael, Tyler, and Kyle, you guys make me a proud Mop.

A special thanks to Nicole Martinez with Crescent Moon Miniatures & Artistry for bringing our yappy apple to life with her creative and original artwork, and also to Angie Powell for her patience and amazing editorial talent.

ENDNOTES

1. Captain Chelsey "Sully" Sullenberger, interview by Katie Couric, February 8, 2009, television, "60 Minutes", CBS News.

RECOMMENDED READING

The Educator's Diet:
 Teaching with 21st Century Recipes
Carol Woodard

The 7 Habits of Highly Effective People
Dr. Stephen R. Covey

"Will Power", *Chicago Tribune,*
Staff Writer Wes Smith, published June 13, 1995

"There's Nothing Wrong with Your Legs"
joelosteen.com, published Sept 12, 2014

Way of the Peaceful Warrior
Dan Millman

Switch on Your Brain
Dr. Caroline Leaf

Man's Search for Meaning
Viktor Frankl

QBQ
John G Miller

ABOUT THE AUTHOR

Carol Woodard

Carol is the former Chairperson for Career Educators Alliance (CEA), and has served as the Executive School Director and Education Director for a large private school in Texas. As CEO of Yappy Carol, her public speaking engagments have gained international attention, and she has been featured in "O, the Oprah Magazine" as an education expert. Carol has also been published multiple times in "BeautyLink Magazine" among other publications. She is also the author of the groundbreaking book, "The Educator's Diet: Teaching With 21st Century Recipes".

Reach out to Carol directly for more information on Yappy Carol's upcoming events.

Email: Carol@yappycarol.com
Website: https://speakercarol.com
817-999-5959

Notes

Notes

Notes

Notes

Notes

Notes

Notes

Notes

Notes

Notes

Made in the USA
Columbia, SC
10 June 2025